IS

A Journey that will Change your Life

IS
A Journey that will Change your Life

Sandeep Amar

PRABHAT
PRAKASHAN

Published by
PRABHAT PRAKASHAN PVT. LTD.
4/19 Asaf Ali Road,
New Delhi-110 002 (INDIA)
e-mail: prabhatbooks@gmail.com

ISBN 978-93-5266-843-4
IS A JOURNEY THAT WILL CHANGE YOUR LIFE
by Shri Sandeep Amar

Edition
2025

Price
₹ 200.00 (Rupees Two Hundred only)

Printed at
Print Media, New Delhi

Dedicated to
my wife
and
daughter

Preface

It is important to note that language is limited in terms of expression. It is difficult to express experiences in language. While reading the book, you may get a feeling that the language is not correct, or the meaning is not clear. Please try to comprehend and the meaning will be clear. If you keep reading till the end, you will be able to fathom the complete meaning.

It is important that you read the book slowly, seriously and carefully. And likewise use your own life experiences to interpret and understand the assertions made in the book. I hope you enjoy reading the book.

Yours Truly,
Sandeep Amar

Contents

1
The Relative and the Absolute

"The Moment is"

The first two concepts we need to understand are "absolute" and "relative."

The "absolute" is the entire creation of nature, and not of human thought. The trees, the mountains, the rivers and the seas are the examples of "absolute". Humans are also created as "absolute." But the human thought perceives it as "relative" in terms of superior, inferior and so many other things.

It is difficult to describe the "absolute", as "it is," here "it is" means that "it is there as a reality". The "absolute" is. The last sentence is complete in the real sense. The absolute has no purpose and no comparison. The mountains, the seas have no purpose, no goal and no comparison. Only human beings have given them names and meanings. Otherwise, these natural assets are not made for humans or owned by humans. The Mount Everest is a name given by humans, and it is part of a country called Nepal is also created by humans.

But that is not the "absolute" truth. The "absolute" cannot be judged, and there is no meaning that can be drawn out of it. The "absolute" is existential and experiential. It is there, not as per human sensory experience, it is there as it is.

The "absolute" is not created by a human being. The "absolute" is created by Nature. The only way to understand the "absolute" is to be one with it. All of us experience it almost every day; there are moments of indulgence in it. As an example, one is near a massive mountain or watching a sunset or looking at a child, your thoughts disappear for a few moments, in these moments you experience the absolute.

Then the thoughts come to mind and, the experience is over. You may indulge in the "absolute" in a moment, in the next moment you interpret it and the "absolute" disappears. The "absolute" cannot be questioned, it has no logic, yet it is the only existence. We will revisit this again and again and try to comprehend the "absolute" to the fullest.

The "relative" can be anything; it may be described in any amount of words. The "relative" depends on the reference frame. The "relative" is there as you are there. Thought creates it, thought of one person. The thought will always be, of one person, and it will still be "relative". There can be millions of physical reference frames – like while looking outside from a moving train; you may feel that it is the outside which is moving.

But if we think of considering mental reference frames, they can be infinite. The "relative" here can be anything:

1. Wealth
2. Height
3. Weight
4. Looks
5. Size of car
6. Mobile phone
7. Clothes
8. Sex appeal
9. Job
10. Breast size
11. Hair
12. Salary
13. House
14. Friends
15. The list is endless.

With all these "relative" frames we create thoughts of relativity. We regularly compare and compete.

To understand "relative", let us look at some answers to the fundamental questions about the "relative". These answers are the most straightforwardly possible explanation of facts as we know them.

What is "relative" in simple terms?

It is the comparative metric, as per the reference frame. The genesis of the reference frame is the individual mind of a human being.

Who is the reference frame?

You are the reference frame. Our mind is the one, which creates the comparison and the competition.

Who are you?

You are the ability to express and interpret

what you sense (see, hear, etc.) in a structured model called mind.

This model is based on your ability to sense the stimulus as per your awareness levels, its assimilation into long term and short term memory, the ability to derive logic from that, in turn, to further sense and interpret the stimulus.

This expression and interpretation happens in the form of thoughts, which forms logic systems (like values and beliefs) for further examinations. In the mechanical world, your consciousness is the expression of this structured model called mind.

What are your reference metrics?

Your reference metrics are the benchmarks as per you, on which you compare things, people, environment, and circumstances outside of you.

What is outside of you?

It seems like the simplest of all questions, but it is not; we will investigate it later.

How do you build your reference metrics?

You build your reference metrics from the model of mind. The judgment happens by these parameters. You create these metrics from your perception (derived from social conditioning) of stimulus as you breathe.

What is "as you breathe"?

As you breathe is the depiction of you as a living human being. This representation cannot be done regarding time, as for now, we will that assume time does not exist. As we go along, you can have your definition of time.

How do you learn?

You learn as you interpret and comply to be a part of the civilised society, where you are born.

The learning is a collection of thoughts bundled with beliefs, values, etc. In the neurons, these values and beliefs are created as per perception to facilitate oneself in so-called future. These are conscious and unconscious choices of the brain or the safety mechanisms as defined by psychologists. Progressively, this is the attempt to be like the world one sees around oneself. This training is just like training of dogs, by rewarding them for specific activities. We train our younger ones, and we encourage them when they imitate the acceptable norms of civilised society.

What is perception?

It is the way we interpret the senses. In a way, it is our interpretation data analytics software, which analyses the sensory data and provides us with the interpretation.

It is based on historical data; it is non-intuitive and dependent on the "relative" frame of reference. It does not consider anything outside the historical information, works on only the data it has captured. The software is dynamic, and as it collects data, it keeps updating the interpretation. There is also something called collective perception, which becomes an accepted form of interpreting data for each society.

What is thinking?

It is the ability to produce a chemical change called "thought." This chemical change is the lifeblood of the model of existence for a human being. The "thought" is an expression or interpretation, and the process is called thinking. The words of the famous economist Keynes "Thinking makes it so!"

defines the impact of thinking in the best manner. He has talked about how thinking drives demand (expected demand theory). In fact, thought controls everything in the human civilization. Even if we try to understand what is thinking? It will be done with thinking. The thought is always "relative".

Let us move on from the fundamental questions and answers. One observation we can make is that "relative" is a lot of interpretation and analysis or a 'lot of thinking.' The more "relative" frames you have, the more thinking models and patterns you tend to develop. When you create many models for many reference frames, there is a continuous analysis and interpretation in the brain. This constant activity of brain becomes a habit.

To merely understand, we keep thinking, comparing, planning and evaluating the models of references frames. We keep adding new models of reference regularly. Generally, they are categories and sub-categories of the primary reference criteria we have set. For example, wealth comparison is a favorite reference in the world.

Wealth comparison is done by comparing houses, cars, home furnishings, clothes, parties, bags and so on. So the primary reference criterion is "wealth comparison" or "affluence comparison," and the surrogates which are categories and sub-categories are defined above. On the primary measure, we keep building the categories and sub-categories.

With various criterions, we create models to tackle, what is termed as "situations" in life. To better understand this, let us take an example of travel, and how people compare vacations or travel with each other. They may look at other people's vacation photos on social media or have a one on one discussion about vacation. There is an instant comparison. If one is less travelled, and someone talked about his/her many vacations, one may feel smaller in life. Thus, slowly one starts becoming sensitive about these situations, and tries to adopt a methodology to "win the situations". We get absorbed in these past, present, and future "situations".

For the past situations, we keep thinking about actions we could have taken, which we did not take at that time. For future cases, we keep planning if we will be in a specific situation, how are we going to manage it?

These situations are created as a result of "relative" comparison, and we may keep thinking about these situations. It becomes a complicated web of thought patterns, relating to pleasure or pain from these situations. This is a constant crisis, which keeps us in pain.

The next point to understand is that the "relative" is the backbone of our social life. Without the "relative" frames, we will be left with nothing much to think or talk. The day will go with few basic sentences like "I want to get some food," or "I am going to work." Even thoughts will be very less as there is little to think about without the "relative". A bus is a bus, a car is a car, and a house is a house.

In "relative", there is so much to do, so much to think, interpret and in turn elongate the event. The "relative thinking" is the food for thought, which is the core the process of mind. That is the reason for the mind to encourage the "relative thinking". The social world is also about the "relative"; the entire social ecosystem is based on the relative comparison of tangibles and intangibles. The social dialogue is based on "relative", and without the "relative", there is little to talk about in day to day life.

Is "relative" right or wrong? Let us not judge it for now.

The "absolute" is your fundamental nature, like getting hungry is "absolute", you do not have to produce a thought for it. You are in the "absolute" many times each day, as soon as the thought enters, it becomes "relative". As explained earlier the process of mind also prefers the "relative"; it creates a lot of brain activity.

One may claim that "relative" is how we work? All the development that happens is based on "relative"; if there is no relative thinking, there will be no work done. Someone in "absolute" state, may be good for nothing. The "relative" runs the world, the competition is the name of the game, and all progress is due to that.

This perception that the work and development happen due to "relative" is a big misconception. All progress has happened and will further occur by an understanding of the "absolute". The "absolute" is. It means the "absolute" is there, and it is not there because human race thinks so! It is independent of human's ability to think. The presence of stars, planets, galaxies, rivers, mountains, animals is not due to any human intervention.

The cities and buildings are built out of human thought, but not the rivers and the seas. The first significant progress for the humans was learning how to farm. Hunting was instinct, but farming was learning, the learning of how plants grow. The growth of plants is an "absolute" phenomenon. The skill of agriculture was the first step towards civilisation.

Only post invention of farming, people started living together near agricultural land and river beds. In a way, this formed the basis of civilisation and society. Right from the Einstein's theories to Darwin's theories, they are all about understanding the "absolute". Here is a quote from Einstein himself, which may clarify the point better:

"A human being is a part of the whole, called by us the "Universe," a part limited in time and space. He experiences himself, his thoughts and feelings as something separated from the rest, a kind of optical delusion of his consciousness. This delusion is a kind of prison for us, restricting us to our personal desires and to affection for a few persons closest to us."

As per the quote, the experience of the self is the delusion, that delusion is similar to what has been defined here as "relative."

Any scientific creation and discovery are not achieved through the past learning. Otherwise, it will not be called an "invention." It is the intuitive, not the memory – which creates this invention, which is the nature of the "absolute", not the "relative". We will understand and investigate this in later chapters.

So the understanding of "absolute" provides the real progress. The "relative" is human creation, it can have any meaning as one individual mind may perceive. There is collective conditioning as well, where a certain set of people in a particular geography, or part of a sect or religion start following certain norms. That is just a human creation, and little meaning in the "absolute" reality of life and existence.

As an example, every day we see new products and services are launched in the market. The 'advertising' tries to persuade the consumers to buy these items or services. The 'advertising' tries to tell us, how we should live, what is a more comfortable situation for us, generally that is the situation shown after the consumer has bought their product or service. Advertising tries to create collective conditioning. Similarly, media and social media also creates collective conditioning.

This psychosis is enhanced by adding new elements and new terms, which were previously not there. Therefore people would want to achieve these new elements. These elements can be new services, new products, new uses of old products or services, new social media platforms, a new way of taking photos (example: taking selfies), a new image in front of friends on Facebook and many such things. It is encouraged to learn and discuss new products and services, and final objective is to own these new things.

Please investigate this carefully; we are just fueling our psychosis. We are trying to take actions, which makes us "look good" in our reference group.

And the definition of making us "look good" keeps changing, from which we can conclude that it is all just an unending race. The problem begins when one reaches the so-called objectives and then makes new ones. It is a vicious cycle, a cycle of constant longing, anxiety, and pain.

These are walls, we have created on our own. Next step is to seek relief, relief from this constant state of pain. Most of this pain is just created out of conditioning and perception, but the pain is real.

The model of mind creates this psychosis, which originates from the "relative" frames. The resulting pain pushes us, to get pleasure but in the same structure. For example, if one is comparing one's car with a friend's car, and the friend's car is a more expensive car. One experiences the pain of being left behind, and the solution to that is somehow own an even better (or more expensive) car.

It is the cycle we have accepted, and one may say life has ups and downs. It is not life, it is us who have created these ups and downs as per our interpretation which is driven by societal conditioning.

We don't make choices; we think we do, but we don't. People think they have an opportunity to make choices if they have money, and that gives them an option. The material world runs on this philosophy; it seems that money will provide for freedom, security, and opportunity.

The concept of choice is understood like buying flavours at an ice-cream parlour. If you have the money, you can buy any flavour. But the choice does not mean this. The choice has two dimensions. The first aspect of choice is about being the master and not the slave. Choice means that you have complete control over your decision, and you use your personal decision rather than being influenced by societal conditioning.

If someone abuses you, you immediately feel bad. But you have a choice; you may choose not to feel bad about it. Once you feel you have a choice to feel bad or not to feel bad, then you are in the first dimension of choice.

The "second dimension of choice" can only come if you are in the first dimension. The second dimension of choice is to choose to be in the "relative" or the "absolute" consciously. To further understand, it is the choice to be in the "world created by human thought" or the world "as it is" (not created by human thought).

Sometimes we experience a lot of pain; all of us get to that point, where we get sick of life and our mental psychosis. When we are in extreme pain, pain becomes a constant reality; we are not able to get out of that misery. Now in these situations, we can see the pain, and then we can see the psychosis as an external entity.

Let us understand it further; the extreme pain pushes us to understand pain – that pain exists, and we cannot run away from it. It becomes a new way to look at the pain, in extreme pain – we see pain! Every once in a while we lose hope and see only pain.

When we see pain and are ready to feel the pain, we can see the cause of the pain as an entity which may be the mental psychosis.

It is not the extreme pain; it is the philosophy to tackle the pain that makes the difference. The pain is tackled through hope; hope that things will get better. Now, this becomes a roadblock in understanding pain; hope relieves the pain.

This does not mean hope and positive thinking is wrong. But by covering up the pain with hope, the mechanics of pain are not understood.

Once the pain is examined, this state can be a state of awareness. Please note that this does not mean that awareness can only be achieved through pain, actually being aware is our true nature. Looking into pain is a sure way of getting into a state of awareness.

Awareness is the first state to reach as only from here can we exercise choice, otherwise we have no choice.

If you are not in the "state of awareness" you cannot lead a life of choice. In today's mad world, this state may only be achieved once you are in extreme pain due to living in mental psychosis. The examination of extreme pain can show you how the mind is the enemy. Once you can see that "the mind is the enemy," that is the surrogate of awareness.

The state of awareness is the first step; it is the door to anything that has to come next. As soon as you are aware, you are no longer in pain, and you can choose to rip apart the walls which are choking you. Awareness is the state of zero; it is like you are going through brochures of products and making a conscious decision. The awareness provides you with the ability to make choices.

If you are prepared for it, the awareness will come. In the modern world, the preparation for this is the pain. If you do not feel any pain in life, you may already be aware, or you are in the "relative" frame.

Therefore, pain is good – it forms a gateway to get out of this psychosis. But for some, the psychosis is the reality, and they do not experience pain.

The people who think there is something wrong in their lives, there is some emptiness in their lives, some amount of pain, feel the need to break the inertia. You may have set some objectives for yourself, post reaching those objectives, if you don't feel fulfilled, and the pain remains, please note that you may be looking for the "absolute".

For others who feel they have reached somewhere, they are not ready for the "absolute". They are the players of the "relative", they have set targets in the "relative" world, and they reached them and are satisfied. They will always be players, never be spectators. In this domain, being a spectator is important – the game is irrelevant. For the players of the "relative" frame – the life is a "delusion" which Einstein has referred to as "is a kind of prison for us."

Only the people with pain feel the prick of the delusion, and they may reach awareness to get into a state of "making a choice."

In the state of awareness, you are empowered to make a choice. It is like looking in the mirror carefully, just look at your face and your existence there at that moment. Your awareness of being there is what you have forgotten. The choice is to take action. The choice is whether to react or not to react to the psychosis. The choice is whether to interpret or not to interpret. The choice is to stay as a watcher rather than a player in action.

The watcher does not mean that there is no action; the watcher implies that there is no interpretation of the action. From here you may know how to be in the "absolute".

The sentence sounds incorrect, due to limits of language, but it is correct. You and "absolute" are the same, you are a part of it, and it is the whole. So you cannot move into it, you are in it. You only have to know that you are in it. You have to see each moment that you are in it. Each moment is important, each moment you have to see that you are in it. The moment is the key; it is the "absolute". The moment is the "absolute". The "absolute" is. The moment is.

Summary

The Moment is.

2
The Continuous and the Discontinuous

"The awareness is, the time is not"

The awareness empowers us to make choices. We need to be in the moment, and we need to be aware, then we will have the power of choice. Let's look at the next steps from there.

At this moment, the moment of awareness, one is aware of the self, the individual self. It is not a magical experience; it is just awareness that I am there and there are things around me. It is just like when the rain and clouds are gone, and the sunlight is back, it becomes clear. We need to explore what is 'I' and the other (other than 'I', the things around me). The things around "I" or other than "I" may be considered as the entire universe. Although "I" am also part of it, but for now "I" is a spectator, so we study the universe. We need to explore the functioning of the world.

The world seems continuous, but if observed carefully it is discontinuous. It looks continuous as per our sensory (see, hear, etc.) experience. Our senses give an impression of things being continuous.

What we see through the eyes is continuous, all motion seems continuous. Let us understand how "if observed carefully" it is discontinuous.

It is like in mathematics and statistics if you are asked what comes after 1, you may say 2. But after 1, there is 1.01 or 1.001 or 1.0001 and so on going up to infinity. In statistics, there is an underlying assumption that the data is continuous. But as we saw in the example data is discontinuous. Similarly, when we see things, hear things, and feel things, we sense that they are continuous. It is the limited ability of our senses that make things appear continuous. But if we observe them they may appear discontinuous.

There was a significant scientific debate on this, in the early 20th century. The discussion was on Quantum Theory, which explained the world as random and discontinuous, and it stands to be the most accepted theory today as well. The argument was refuted by Einstein and some of his fellow scientists. They published a paper called the EPR (Einstein, Podolsky, and Rosen) paradox.

Einstein also made the famous comment "God does not play dice" indicating whatever God has made is definite and not random or discrete. It is worth looking at the bottom line of what science has found about the working of the universe.

We may start with the theories of Newton, which is known as classical or Newtonian mechanics. This mainly consisted of the laws of motion and the theory of gravitation. He explained all the movements in the universe right from the fall of the apple to the orbiting of the planets.

The laws of motions say that a state of motion or a state of rest tends to stay as it is unless an external force is applied, the motion is proportional and in the direction of the force applied, and every action has an equal and opposite reaction.

The law of gravitation suggested that there is a force of gravity amongst all bodies and directly proportional to mass and inversely proportional to the distance between them.

This just means all bodies attract each other, the higher their masses, the higher the pull, and the lower the distance between the distance between them, the higher the pull and vice versa.

He explained that the planets are orbiting around the sun due to the gravitation pull of the sun. Here is an interesting quote from him:

"Gravity explains the motions of the planets, but it cannot explain who set the planets in motion. God governs all things and knows all that is or can be done."

Newton here tries to explain how he has only described the functioning of the universe, but not the genesis of operation. What he has described is merely the first how of "how things work" but how they started to work is not known. It may only be known to the one who started it. It is important to understand, that when we look at scientific explanations of the universe, they are just focused on how things are happening, and not on why is it like that and who/what started it.

Newton has indicated this gap. At the same time, let us not get into how things are governed by God or by anything else, but we will keep this question in mind and will take it up later.

Newton's theories were considered to be the biggest revolution in science, and it was the most accepted theory by scientific community till Einstein came out with the Theory of Relativity.

In the late 19th century a lot of experiments were coming out with results which were not in accordance with Newton's theory.

To explain this new data, Einstein came about with his theory of relativity in 1905 followed up by another version of it in 1915. The theory is not a straightforward proposition to be understood in one paragraph, and cannot be illustrated easily like Newton's assertions. So we will just try to understand a part which is feasible in general. He gave the speed of light, which is the fastest speed that can be achieved. According to him, the speed of light is a constant and rest of the motion in the universe can be seen relative to that.

He gave the famous equation of E = mc2 which illustrates the relationship between energy and mass, and more importantly that they are inter-convertible, or they are one. He gave several seemingly complicated assertions like gravity being a curving of space-time and the concept of time dilation in which the clocks in a fast moving frame go slow. The only thing to gather here is that space and time are related. The space-time curving is responsible for the earth and other planets orbiting around the sun. Also, the same phenomenon explains rest of the universe. Here let's not get into space-time and its explanation, we can just gather that this is a new way of describing the same phenomenon like gravity, motion, etc.

The next theory is called the Quantum Theory. "Quantum" a word derived from quanta which is how light (and energy) travel in packets called quanta. These packets called quanta are like particles, an assertion is given by Einstein himself about light.

The quantum theory came into the picture to explain the atomic world, which Einstein's Relativity Theory was not able to. The basis of the Quantum Theory is the Uncertainty Principle, which says that position and velocity of a particle cannot be found simultaneously (Heisenberg's Uncertainty Principle). Now, this essentially means our instruments are not good enough to deduce it.

Therefore, what best we can do is to use probability to find where they could be, but their path of moving from one place to another is not known. It is essential to think about, at that time the scientists who gave the theory were themselves not entirely convinced of it. But the mathematical model was correct as it was based on the probability of events happening. In simple words, the path and position of subatomic particles cannot be found. This may sound somewhat stupid logic, but this is the most accepted theory of the universe today by the scientific community.

The Quantum Theory indicates that there is randomness, and only discrete or discontinuous scenarios can be predicted by using mathematical equations of probability. Now, this is different from the Newton's and Einstein's assertions, in which everything is precise and continuous. In Quantum Theory, everything is discrete, discontinuous and uncertain (we can only find probability).

As explained earlier Einstein challenged the theory and said that God has made everything definite and God does not play dice.

Let us look at it again. This is what Einstein was saying – that there may be many paths which a sub-atomic particle may take (to move from one point to another). We may find probabilities of the same, but in reality, it has taken one path, which is continuous and absolute. Quantum Theory says the path cannot be known, as it is uncertain, so the probability is the best choice.

You may follow any of the assertions, but hopefully, you get the confusion and point of debate. It is like asking "is motion continuous?" The answer may seem yes! But Quantum Theory says no! If an object has to move from one point to another it has to pass through the millions of points in the middle, and as per Quantum Theory how are we sure that it passed through all the points? So it is discontinuous, the motion can be defined as an object at different locations at different times.

If we look at the world, if we observe it, the world is discontinuous. The key reason for that is the way we look at the world, it is moment to moment, which is a discrete way of looking. The reason for that is "awareness is discrete." The awareness is always at the moment; therefore, the world will be seen as discrete or discontinuous. Awareness is from moment to moment – consequently discrete.

Now let us look closely at the assertions. First, as we observe the world or anything, it is discontinuous.

This "as we observe" has to be understood, it means as we visually inspect the surrounding. We see the room, the park, the house visually, and then we see it again in next moment and then again and again.

This looks like a continuous process, but it is not, as our awareness is discrete. Now it is not because the world is dynamic and it is changing. You may have heard the famous Zen saying that "you cannot step in the same river twice." But the discontinuity is not because the world is dynamic; it is because the awareness is discontinuous. The awareness happens in steps when you watch, you look and look and look, each look is different, and the world may be same or different. Now, this can only be experienced and cannot be written in words.

Taking up from where we left, the first step of any progress is awareness.

Let us consider that awareness is discrete. As you are in a state of awareness, you see the world in discrete frames. You can distinguish one moment from the next. When we are not in a state of awareness, the world looks continuous. There seems to be no space in thoughts or the observation of the world. The world appears continuous; instead, we don't even think if it is continuous or not. Everything seems connected, this happened, and that happened and so on.

We are either in past or the future. Life seems to have no break as we live today, thinking about the future or the past, which creates constant anxiety. We are generally looking for a break. Everyone says "I need a break." This is the most genuine question of humanity today "mankind needs a break." But for the majority of us, a break means an escape. It is a break from doing what we do not like to do.

The state of awareness helps a person to take a "break." Awareness makes sure everything stops, and a person in the state of awareness enters the present. In the state of awareness, the break is experienced. In the state of awareness, time disappears, therefore it is a break.

As you watch the world in awareness, your breathing stays is the only reality. The next step could be any of the following two, which we will take up in later chapters:

1. You may continue to enjoy the state of awareness.

2. You may get thoughts and move back to non-awareness in the world of societal self-image, the world of relative.

We will investigate these movements later. We have bypassed the question of time in the first chapter.

Let us look at it now. Time is the surrogate for motion. That is why we say time has passed. It signifies something that has happened; it is a representation of the verb. It is physically signified from the rising to the setting of the sun, which constitutes a day and space in the middle.

The collection of days is made into weeks, months and years. The collection of days into a year constitutes one revolution of the earth around the sun. So the physical time as we know it is the mapping of motion of the earth around the sun.

But we know very well the sun does not set or rise. We know it is just an illusion since we have the earth as the reference frame. Therefore, the first thing we can immediately conclude is that this human concept of time regarding different units is not the universal concept, as we are just looking at the motion of our planet, around a star.

Now let us move further and ask if there is a universal concept of time. Again the answer will be no as there are so many motions in the universe. Therefore, there cannot be a question of single time.

The next question is – does time exist? Is the thing called time really there? The answer is again no. There is no real thing as time. Empirically time is there as a concept, but that is only in a relative physical frame. Otherwise, time does not exist. The idea of time is a facilitator for our living as a social being on earth. You can ask any scientist, and he/she will agree that time does not exist. But you ask him/her in day to day life to forget time, throw away all the clocks, they will not.

For every human being time as a concept is one of the most important ideas in life. Time is significant, we do not want to waste time, we want to utilise it. The utilisation of time should be "productive", like the saying "time is money".

For us, time exists and is the critical component of our day to day life. The whole planning is based on time, in the absence of time what is the plan? All the thoughts you had today are based on the concept of time, you only think in the time frame, enjoying or ruing the past, or anticipating the future, or living in the present. Time is everything when it comes to the functioning of mind, the whole operation of mind and thought creation and its complete psychosis is based on time.

The whole societal conditioning is based on time, that you have to plan to be more successful, for which there is a definition for the future, which we need to pursue. The perusal is for our societal dream, for our ideal state and we have to reach there.

The mind has its tricks, to keep us involved in similar thoughts, these tricks are based on the concept of time. All in all, whatever anyone says about time, we may be entirely convinced it exists, that's the base of our thoughts, which is mostly our life.

We may read hundreds of articles by eminent physicists citing Quantum Theory and other theories that time does not exist. But even own their human brain as an individual may believe in time in the day to day life.

So let us consider that time exists. Since we know time is not real, so it is a creation of society and our mind.

This concept of time is continuous. There is no break in this concept of time in the mind. We plan continuously; we live in a time trap, this trap is endless. This goes on and on and on. Since it is a continuous track, one may need a break from it. As described earlier, one may confuse this break for an escape.

Remember you can fool the self, but you cannot kill the person. The self seeks a break, this is a genuine question of self, the nature of the self is not continuous, so it needs a break.

The concept of time lends us almost all the thoughts we think in a day. These thought patterns are continuous and seek an unlimited continuity. This continuity needs to be understood very carefully.

This continuity may be understood with a small example from an incident with Lao Tzu. Once Lao Tzu was with two people looking at the sunset, one of them was his friend, and the other was someone known to his friend. This third person (the person known to his friend) said, "the sunset is so beautiful". Lao Tzu told his friend that his friend was very talkative. Now what Lao Tzu indicated was about continuity. The indication was that the sunset was beautiful, they were aware of it and were enjoying looking at it. But by talking about it, we want to extend it, extend the feeling. We sought continuity in the sunset, which was giving pleasure.

We take pictures to capture our moments, to relive the past, to experience the nostalgia. Now the habit of the mind cannot be one dimensional; the continual nature lends the same effect to bad things that happen to us. We stay heavily conditioned by both negative and positive experiences.

It is like being afraid of going to the street, where we had an accident. If you had an accident in one street, as we get near that same street we feel the same fear. This is continuity. This fear may become more or less over time, depending on what is occupying your mind over time. The reality is that the accident most probably will not happen again, and every situation is a new situation and should not have the baggage of the old situation.

Still, due to continuity, our brain brings back the fear.

But what Lao Tzu is trying to say is that see the sunset as it is there, the joy of watching it is inherent, you need not express it. The idea of expression is the idea of continuity, which will lead to conditioning. You will tell this to someone else, "I saw a great sunset", then the next sunset you see, you may say "this is not as good as the last one".

The continuity is not about expression of thoughts, as in the Lao Tzu story, but about the extension of thoughts, it is about the extension of joys and sorrows, it is about extending one moment to another. We need to remember one moment is different from the other. The moments are discrete; our mind tries to treat them as continuous.

So from the concept of time, comes the concept of continuity and from the concept of continuity comes to the idea of conditioning. The conditioning is the baggage of one moment over the other. The idea that we try to get continuity from one moment to another, for all the experiences, we get conditioned for the moment to come.

The two moments are different, but our mind treats everything as continuous, so it carries the baggage of one moment to the next. We see the world with glasses of conditioning. We create this conditioning every moment, the experience of every moment adds more conditioning.

The state of awareness is the state in which we see the world in the present moment without any baggage of the previous moment. Since the moments are discrete, the state of awareness is discrete. The discrete state is a state of timelessness. We have understood that in the state of awareness conditioning disappears.

To sum up, time lends the continuity to the mind, time does not exist, the continuity does not exist, in the absence of continuity, conditioning does not exist. But all this happens in the state of awareness. Therefore, the awareness is, the time is not.

Summary

The Moment is.

The awareness is. The time is not.

3
The 'I' and The Other

"The other is not, the 'I' is"

The constant struggle in life brings about a lot of questions – is this world a really tough place to live in? Am I not strong enough? The answer to these questions may be anything, but these issues keep coming back to most of us. One of the solutions to the problems is to create a reference frame and focus on people who are doing worse than you. For example, you refer to a poor(er) guy and thank God that you are doing better than him. But it does not end there. The circle completes when you feel bad, looking at someone who is doing better than you in the same regard. This struggle is created again since comparison and competition is a double-edged sword.

As per our understanding from the last chapter, the logic of mind seeks continuity. Seeking continuity is like tracing a path. And we also understood the discrete nature, which is like tracking different points at a different time. This tracing of the path is what we know as "my life" in the sense of "psychological time," the continuity, the conditioning and the relative nature.

Looking at the "my life" seems like looking at the path, by self, and by others. Children up to a certain age do not trace a path. Children as a matter of existence do not seek continuity; they do not trace the path. As they grow, they are taught to trace the path.

The path is regarding time, events and places. "My life" is represented as "time, events and places." The "time, events and places" is just our physical presence in those dimensions. In each of those "times, events and places," there could have been various possibilities.

We just trace our life as a collection of what happened, and not what other things that could have happened! To extend this, we start looking at the future with a similar framework.

The critical question is "who am 'I'?" It is like when you are eating an apple, and ask yourself "who is eating the apple?" When you are looking in the mirror, you ask yourself "who is looking in the mirror, and whose reflection is in the mirror?" Is 'I' defined by a name, place, date of birth, college and school, parents, and profession?

The simple answer to these questions is that "'I' am here and now, so what is the next thing 'I' should do?" This may be considered a good answer. This answer gets you to be here and now. Now if one is asked a question about yesterday's match or tomorrow's lunch appointment, it will take the person to past or future – and a chain of thoughts will be created.

The question about 'I' seems like a good question, it is a question in the present tense and brings a person to present (as in now). You can try this small exercise and keep asking these questions about 'I,' and you will realize that the questions are bringing you to the present. It is an important and fundamental question. But for now, we can use it as a trick. The trick is to be aware – how little one is thinking about oneself!

To define "my life," we try to trace a path of "time, events and places" of what has happened and keep thinking of what could have happened. We need to understand 'I,' who is constant in "my life," who was there in all "time, events and places." Therefore the key question is "Who am 'I'?"

If we go a little deeper, the first question could be "is this voice inside me is the real me, or am 'I' something else?" The second question could be "Is there just one voice or two voices or more than two?" People say the two voices are heart and mind, one voice is of heart, and one is of the mind. Is that really correct? Let us check it out, let us just close our eyes and use one voice to tell the other voice to speak up.

The result could be that no one speaks up and if one waits a bit longer – you hear a voice, but was it the first voice which just moved to the other side?

This needs a lot of work, but questions about 'I' bring you in the present and in awareness of "your presence." Being aware of "oneself being here right now" may sound silly but it is the most important beginning. We may stay with this learning, and the question "Who am I?" and I am aware of myself right here right now.

This is a discrete state, "right here right now state". There is no tracing the path, one is here and one is aware of it. There is nothing relative; one is here right now, one is looking at it – one is the "absolute".

Therefore, you are here and now, looking at your surroundings. You are not moving – you are still, just using your senses to look, hear, smell, etc. Ideally, now everything around you should look like the screen of a movie. You see the world around you like a movie. Imagine, you are here, and you are watching a movie. You are looking at, hearing, and sensing "the other". "The other" is passing around you and you are here. We think that we are passing the world since we are ageing in terms of chemical changes and degeneration of the body. But it is the other way round; the world is passing, happening like a movie in front of you.

Am 'I' the centre of universe and world is floating around me? Sorry no, no one should think like that – as that is just our ego talking. The point is that the world is transitory and 'I' is permanent. There are a lot of assertions against this, a lot of wise men have said 'I' is transitory and the world is permanent. This needs to be understood.

The only real thing you know is "you." The rest is an apparition. Sunrise and sunset do not happen; the earth is not flat, you can never know what other person is thinking or feeling, you cannot say for sure if a thing is hot or cold till you touch it. You are the only real thing you know. So how can you be transitory? Just try this, stand up and walk, pick up a bike and pedal, start your car and press the accelerator – are you in motion or is the world in motion? In simple terms, you matter the most.

What is other than "you" or 'I'? It is my interpretation of the other. My understanding comes from my mind, which works in a relative frame and seeks continuity.

Therefore, you can never really say with surety what the other is. Just like you can never guess accurately what another person is thinking, similarly the other can be at best an interpretation of mind. The interpretation of mind is conditioned, relative and traces the path of time; it cannot be trusted.

It is a simple matter, when you see ice and when a person from Iceland sees the ice, there may be a difference of interpretation. The interpretation cannot be an absolute fact. Therefore, it has little meaning. Although this should be understood, but even if there is some doubt – let's move ahead with a consideration that the other cannot be known.

The only thing you can know is you, yourself, which we are also calling 'I' here. To know oneself, one has to inquire with questions like "who am 'I'?" and other questions we have discussed before. As soon as these questions appear, awareness appears, time disappears, and the other disappears. These questions bring you in the discrete frame; you are no longer tracing the path, you are enquiring about the only absolute you can know, which is you, yourself. Therefore, the other is not, the 'I' is.

Summary

The Moment is.	
The 'I' is.	The awareness is.
The other is not.	The time is not.

❐

4
The Experience of Experience

"The explained is not. The experience is"

Continuing from the last chapter, we can move towards knowing the 'I'. We can never be sure about the other. We can call it the "uncertainty principle" for the other. If "who am 'I'?" is the right question, what is the answer? Maybe another question – how can one know the 'I'? What is the process for that?

In a famous TV series MASH, there is a character called Charles Emerson Winchester the III and the lead character is nicknamed Hawkeye. Hawkeye and Charles share the same tent in a mobile army hospital during the war in Korea. One day someone asks Hawkeye, "Can you tell me something about Charles," Hawkeye replies "Charles cannot be explained, Charles has to be experienced." That was a joke on Charles since Charles was a very typical personality. So is everyone in the world.

Everyone in the world is typical and unique – it is not related to being superior. Now you are unique, but you have understood yourself as part of some herd. In the relative frame and due to social conditioning – over time you brand yourself as a personality. It may be introvert, extrovert, funny, geeky, serious, aggressive and so on. You also start referring to it in situations; you say "Look I am a sensitive person" or "emotional person" or "an alpha male" and so on.

Everyone does that since it is easy to explain, and it gives us a certain character which we can use in different situations. It may provide acceptance as being part of a group or general understanding of oneself.

This branding of oneself, takes a person away from fundamental questions like "who am 'I'?" This personality type identification and acceptance makes a person accept pain and live in misery, claiming that this is due to his personality. The recognition of pain also prevents exploration of pain – which is very important as we understood in earlier chapters.

To start the process of knowing oneself, the first step is to drop the stereotype, which one has accepted about oneself. Therefore, you are not an introvert, extrovert, geek, emotional, sensitive, insensitive or whatever you think or others might say. Just drop the stereotype for a few days.

Why only a few days? Please understand this; we are all controlled by the mind, which has great power. If you try to take any long-term measures, the mind will not let you take it. It will convince you otherwise, by creating scenarios and illusions. Therefore, everything will be done in baby steps. So if you commit that I am going to do this for two days, the mind does not fight any change for two days.

The first step is to drop the stereotype for two days. The second step is to announce an investigation into oneself. Just announce in your mind, I am going to drop the stereotype for two days and conduct an inquiry about myself.

The third step is to start an investigation using the questioning method. In the questioning method, you will ask for an explanation for each thought that comes.

Let's understand how to do this. Suppose you are a man doing this – you see a girl on TV, on the street, or in a magazine and thought of attraction comes in your mind. Immediately ask these questions:

1. What do I want to do with this attraction?
2. What is the meaning of this attraction?
3. If the girl is on TV or a picture of her is in a magazine, she is not even here. I will probably never meet her, what do I want?
4. Do I want to have sex with her or want to touch her face?
5. Is this a feeling of sexual attraction or some kind of love? Is love a big word to use, as I have just seen her for the first time?
6. Am I getting this feeling each time I see a good looking girl? Am I a sex maniac? Is there a problem in my mind or is my sex life bad?

The simple answer that may come is "Hey I am just looking; it has no meaning, just a two-minute attraction – nothing important." Well, that is not good enough. This is the way we fool ourselves. Everything has a source, just try to find it.

Therefore as an exercise for two days, try to answer all the 5-6 random questions you can think of at that point in time. Since we have dropped the stereotype for 2 days, please do not answer "Oh, I am just a guy" or "It's a guy thing".

What are we expecting here? What is going to happen in this exercise? The exercise is just to disturb the method of the mind, the method it uses to create the thoughts.

The fourth step is to identify the moments.with no thoughts. As you ask these random questions – since you disturb the process of mind – you will get some confused moments. In these moments, you will have no thoughts. In general, you just treat these confused moments as traps – and you immediately jump out of these traps. You jump out of the traps by saying, "What am I thinking?", "Oh, stop being stupid," "let's move on, man!" or "Why am I stupid?"

Now we will create these confused moments and try to stay in them as long as possible. When the questions leave you confused, just stay there – although you will get a natural urge to jump out but do not do it. The chaotic moments are signals of mind losing control. Therefore, the fourth step is to identify the confused moments.

The final and fifth step is an attempt to prolong these confused moments. Try and stay in confused moments for as long as possible – these are moments without thoughts. We need to try these steps for two days.

The conclusion of this exercise may be – "I am not what I have accepted myself to be." Therefore the question "Who am 'I'?"

The objective of the exercise is to increase conviction and reason behind knowing oneself or asking the question "Who am 'I'?" This question needs to become stronger and stronger. The answer to this question is experiencing the state with no thoughts. It does not sound like an answer, but for now, let's go with this.

The experience cannot be explained. The explained is not an experience. The experience of state with no thoughts will give a path to the essential thing in life.

The experience of moments with no thought will give a path to the experience of the world through senses. Now in these moments with no thought, one can see with eyes, hear from ears, taste, and smell and feel the air.

The experience of self will give rise to the experience of everything around self. Please note that there is nothing spiritual, magical, mystical or supernatural about this. It is just being natural.

There are no thoughts. Therefore, there is no meaning. There is no meaning to you and there is no meaning about what you are sensing. If you are looking at the TV, you are just looking – you may get a nice feeling but without any thought.

The simple assumption is that you are your mind. But you are there without your mind as well. Therefore, you are.

You are – without mind, without time, without the past, without tracing a path and without the other (people, things). You are there without any of these things. You are not the explanation (introvert, sensitive or insensitive) – as you exist without an explanation as well. Therefore, the explanation is not, the experience is.

Summary

The Moment is.	
The awareness is.	The time is not.
The 'I' is.	The other is not.
The experience is.	The explanation is not.

❐

5
The Self and No-Self

"The 'I' is none. The no – 'I' is one."

The experience of self, opens doors to the experience of the other. If one sees oneself, one sees the other, just like a movie. In the experience, the explanation disappears, senses appear. When the explanation disappears, mind disappears, knowledge disappears, intelligence disappears, and intuition may appear. Please remember intuition is not a scientific or a logical thing, it is a personal thing. The process of experiencing the self and the other facilitates the intuition, but cannot guarantee it.

We were investigating "Who am I?" and related questions, which helped us to get to the confused moments with no thoughts. When we extended these moments, we reached a state of experience of self and the other. We may get the answers during the experience, and these answers are answers of intuition. These may be the correct answers to individual questions.

But what could be the answer to the central question "Who am 'I'?" The answer to this question may be "'I' am alive, 'I' have life in me, and 'I' am life." The answer is correct but sounds very generic. This is an answer for everyone, but we were looking for uniqueness when we asked this question.

Our uniqueness is our intuition, which is personal. Therefore experience will bring intuition, individuality, innovation, and invention. It will answer the unique part, but let's focus on the generic part for now.

'I' am living and 'I' am life. If 'I' am life, then what is the other? The other is life and non-life, which we call as living and non-living. The life or living things are same as 'I' am. The non-living is the one which does not have a life.

Now all livings things are same and must have the same life force in them. There are various scientific theories on the same, starting from a scientist James Hutton. James Hutton in 1785 claimed that Earth is a superorganism.

Another American biologist James Grier in 1978 tried to formulate a living systems theory around how all living things work and the relation between them.

Later in 1991, Robert Rosen, American biologist also described the relation between "part and the whole." Another American ecologist, Robert Ulanowicz has written a book in 2009 – "A Third Window: Natural Life Beyond Newton and Darwin." In this book, he mentions "gaps of science" – wherein he mentions various incomplete theories – and gives meaning to "God of the gaps."

We do not need to get into details of this, we just need to understand that there has been substantial scientific work done on the living systems and this is not a mystical concept.

Therefore even in scientific circles, the living system is well accepted and well researched. We can conclude that all living beings have the same life force. Please do not anticipate that we are moving towards the establishment of God. There is something same in all living beings, and 'I' is one of the living beings. Does this mean everyone is the same? No! We established that everyone is unique and we have to investigate that.

So there is one part which is same, which is the 'life force' and there is a part which is different. The logical thing to deduce is that this different part is the 'I' part, which we are trying to find through the question "Who am 'I'?" We started from this question. The unique part about me is how 'I' am different from other living things or human beings in my case? 'I' is different concerning physical appearance, which is one difference. But what is different about 'I' from the inside?

Most of the differences we can point out are the stereotypes or the social conditioning or the relative comparison. That is not the right answer to "Who am 'I'?" Then the intuition could be the right answer as my intuition is unique, that must be the different part.

But the intuition can only happen in awareness and the experience of self. This only happens when we drop all stereotypes and conditioning. For the world, the 'I' is my name, my job, my money, my house, my hairstyle and so on. Even 'I' is understood by self to be the same. But that is not correct. Therefore that understanding of 'I' is wrong. The 'I' which is different and unique is my intuition, which gets activated when the perception of 'I' created by social conditioning and stereotyping disappears!

To know the real 'I', we have to remove the unreal 'I', which is essentially my social image. As that image is nothing, just an apparition – of my assumptions, defence mechanisms, conditioning and stereotyping. The real 'I' is my intuition. But the real 'I' will appear only when we can drop the fake or social image 'I'.

When we drop this fake 'I' – we have a chance to be the one whom we really are. The chance to activate our true self, our intuition, our individuality. Therefore, the 'I' (conditioning) is not, and no – 'I' is the one.

Summary

The Moment is.	
The awareness is.	The time is not.
The 'I' is.	The other is not.
The experience is.	The explanation is not.
The no – 'I' is the one.	The T (social image) is not.

❐

6
Purpose and No Purpose

"The purpose is not. I am the purpose."

To comprehend from the last chapter, there is a common life force in all of us. And there is something unique in us. The uniqueness is our intuition, our senses and not our name, our job, our house – our social image.

Now how will we find this unique thing in us? The uniqueness appears with awareness and attentiveness. The uniqueness appears with the question "Who am 'I'?" The next question to this question is "What am 'I' doing here?"

"What am 'I' doing here?" relates to my objective of life, my purpose in life. And another related question is "What is the purpose of entire humanity?" Does my life have any meaning? Does the whole human existence have any meaning?

The answer sounds very obvious – Yes!

"What is my purpose" is a question which is very important to tackle. As it carries one of the biggest hidden evil – ego. My purpose could be to take care of my family, my society, my surroundings and so on. My purpose could be to win an Olympic medal, to become a political leader, to be a fighter pilot and so on.

Let us consider for a while that there is no purpose of individual and humanity. If there is no purpose, 'I' has no dimension of importance. 'I' cannot be differentiated from the other. If there is no differentiation, one cannot be more important than the other.

In a world of purpose, there is a leader of the city, there is a leader of the state, and there is a leader of the country. There are hierarchies, and one is more important than the other. In a purposeless world, there are no hierarchies. No one is more important, as there are no criteria to be significant.

No one is useful. When there is no one useful, there is no question of being more or less useful. There is no one skillful; then there is no question of being more and less skillful. There is no one rich; then there is no question of being less or richer.

A world without any purpose – that sounds a bit absurd. There has to be a purpose, if there were no purpose – there would have been no inventions and no progress. Are inventions created by the people who have taken up that purpose or they just happen? The inventors are people on a mission to solve a problem. Solving a problem could be for a purpose or a reason.

When a child looks at the moon for the first time, the child does not even know it is called the 'moon.' Why is it called the 'moon'? Have we asked the name of the 'moon' from 'moon'? The child thinks 'What is that white thing in the sky?' Now the kid wants to 'solve a problem.' That is his or her 'purpose'. That can also be called 'intrigue".

The inventor of polio vaccine, Jonas Salk chose to be in medical research rather than being a practising physician, when asked why? He replied:

"Why did Mozart compose music?"

Here is another quote from him:

"It is always with excitement that I wake up in the morning wondering what my intuition will toss up to me, like gifts from the sea. I work with it and rely on it. It's my partner."

He got excited about virology during his internship and applied for research positions. He worked on flu strains and helped with the development of influenza vaccine. He tested the polio vaccine on himself, his wife and his three sons.

When asked "who owns patent of the vaccine," he replied:

"Well, the people, I would say. There is no patent.

Could you patent the sun?"

Let's study a few more quotes from Jonas Salk:

"Each of us has a different purpose that we have to serve in the evolutionary scheme of things. We are not all equally endowed to do everything. When I speak about teleological evolution, I speak about the idea of "telos," purpose"

"Know the purpose of life that you are inclined to serve, that you are drawn to. Do what makes your heart leap rather than simply follow some style or fashion. Not everyone can or should be a scientist. Not everyone can or should be any one thing. People need to know what kind of purpose they can serve."

If we believe what he is saying, we might conclude that we have a purpose and there is a unique purpose for all of us. This is what we have established in last few chapters. We have also talked about "intuition" and how it helps to solve the problem and have mentioned, "intuition" as his "partner." We have also established the same that the unique part of "I" is intuition.

We may also conclude that scientific invention and growth is not part of a worldly purpose but a byproduct of individual purpose.

We may consider now that the "world has no purpose." There is no purpose of the world, of the society or human beings. Even if there is a world order or a purpose of the world – that is not the purpose of 'I.' The purpose of 'I' is unique.

'I' has a purpose and there is no general purpose at large. Therefore the first step could be to find the purpose of 'I.' And the pretext to that step is that the purpose of 'I' is not aligned with the purpose of the world, as there is no purpose of the world or humankind.

In the Hindu religious book "Bhagwat Gita" – Lord Krishna has explained the purpose of life to Arjuna, the warrior. When Arjuna asked Krishna about the purpose of life, Krishna replied:

"The purpose of life is to be your own self, to be the individual you are supposed to be. This will get you to your designated death."

There is no divine purpose; there is the only individual purpose. In other words, the divine purpose may only be the individual purpose. The individual purpose is not a stated or decided matter. The surrogate of individual purpose is bliss and joy. When one feels bliss and joy, one may be near his or her purpose.

There is a lot of research and analysis about different states of mind – conscious, sub-conscious and unconscious. Here is a quote from the great psychologist Sigmund Freud:

"The poets and philosophers before me discovered the unconscious; what I discovered was the scientific method by which the unconscious can be studied."

There is no conscious, sub-conscious and unconscious. There is just the 'I,' which is singular. With awareness it appears, without awareness, it disappears.

The surrogates of 'I' are joy, bliss, intuitions and sensory experiences. Dr. Freud concluded that the final thing to do is to connect with the "subconscious" and "unconscious", which we are probably referring to as 'I'.

Therefore, the purpose is not. 'I' is the purpose.

Summary

The Moment is.

The awareness is.	The time is not.
The 'I' is.	The other is not.

The experience is.	The explanation is not.
The no – 'I' is the one.	The 'I' (social image) is not.
'I' am the purpose.	The purpose is not.

❐

7

The Happening and The Action

"The growth is not. The "must" is not. The doing is."

The individual purpose will flower with awareness. The individual purpose will open up intuitions and bliss. But is it possible to be in this kind of a frame all the time? Can we be aware all the time?

It is very tough; rather it is impossible to be aware all the time. Actually calling it "to be aware" itself makes it impossible since there is an effort to be aware. The effort can only bring awareness in patches. Therefore, how to make awareness happen?

Awareness is happening all the time! We are in a state which prevents us from experiencing it.

There can be three states – action, inaction, and hypnosis. The action is state of mental or physical work. Inaction is state of contemplation about something. And when contemplation is repetitive, it is hypnosis.

We are mostly in the state of inaction or hypnosis. These are states of planning, anticipation, and collecting–driven by fear, sadness, anxiety, seeking continuity and similar things.

For example, we keep preparing ourselves to manage a situation. It is like thinking "when he will ask this, I will say this or that" and "when the second question comes, I will tackle it this way or that way." If we speak the truth all the time, all this planning and preparation will disappear.

Most of this planning goes to waste as the actual scenario of our anticipation generally does not come true. Even if the situation occurs, we are generally not able to execute the plan.

The important part of understanding is that there is a lot of inaction and hypnosis, which is not providing any great value. Why is there so much inaction and hypnosis? This partly happens due to our concept of purpose, which we derive from the world and society. But as understood earlier that there is no purpose of the world or the society, the purpose is only that of the individual.

We may drop the purpose of the society and the world and focus on "Who am I?" and "What is my purpose?" This can help us get out of hypnosis and inaction. The way of the world is 'growth.' It is similar to what we studied in chapter two, continuity with the concept of time. The purpose of the world goes by the concept of time. This purpose of the world is defined in the form of growth.

When you are a kid, you are supposed to have one kind of 'growth,' when you become young, you are supposed to have some other kind of 'growth.'

This is the reference to stereotypes, which we discarded in chapter five.

The world order says "you must grow." Which we take as "I must grow."

I must grow:

1. as a person
2. in terms of wealth
3. in terms of height
4. in terms of my social life
5. in terms of my job hierarchy
6. .....

In chapter one, we concluded that relative is not. There we compared one thing to another, and on the comparative metric, the "must grow" here is not relative to the other, it is comparable to oneself at different points in life.

There are two words 'must' and 'grow' – which has become a part of the purpose defined by the world and the society. These are the most dangerous words in the world. Here are two quotes from Adolf Hitler:

"A single blow must destroy the enemy... without regard of losses."

"The higher you aspire, the more you grow."

When something 'must' be done, one should not care about the losses. You need to go higher and grow. These are not just words of Hitler; these are words of every nation, every society, and every religion.

Hitler was really serious about it; he was aware of his purpose. Most people consider these actions and get under the pressure of performance and fall into inaction and later hypnosis. Hitler took action and ended up as the architect of the biggest destruction that world has ever seen.

The word 'must' creates a lot of pressure. The words 'grow' or 'growth' creates an ideal state, which is not the present. No state is good enough, we must move to the next state.

If we have bread, we should also have butter! We have butter; we should have cake! We have cake; we should have chocolate cake! And it just goes on.

The ideal state or the best state is never now – there is always the next step. There is always a new objective. Now add the word 'must' to it, 'must grow' or 'must have cake' or 'must have the ideal state.' This 'ideal state' of life, can be realistic until one point. Let us understand this; first needs are food, shelter and clothing. Next is regular income and some savings. Next is savings to last ten years, multiple houses and earning avenues.

My kid should have a personal car, a personal chauffeur, a personal computer and so on. All this is very acceptable.

Chasing this 'ideal state' becomes psychotic, people who become very rich hate the crowd, hate the minor inconveniences. They start wishing for an 'ideal state' in which all perceived inconveniences disappear. One of the nuisances is other people.

I know a wealthy man, one day I invited him to a famous snacks shop – he told me he could go if there were fewer people over there. I told him it is a very crowded shop; he started saying I wish there were fewer people, let me tell my secretary to hire the cook from that snack shop. He just kept going on and on; he said what the purpose of so many people is? Maybe the famines and epidemics were good! At least some of the population problem was resolved. Modern medicine is counterproductive and so on.

I understood the population problem but having little respect for human life for personal comfort is going too far. Hitler went little further than that; he created grand plans for his "ideal state."

His 'ideal state" ideas consisted of a perfect race – people with blue eyes and blonde hair. And the minorities like Jews must die or perish.

Now all of these were apparently psychotic ideas – but these ideas did not happen at once. The more he succeeded at his earlier plans, the more he kept going further and further. The ultimate result was massive destruction, what else could have come out of this!

This whole obsession with the 'ideal state' is the cornerstone of unhappiness. "We must grow," we must move ahead is the motto of the society. Other than a very low percentage of people who can showcase some worldly success, all the others fall victim to this pressure. The first problem is – if I have to succeed I must do it in the right manner. I must plan and anticipate, and due to 'must' – there is anxiety and fear.

When the anxiety and fear increases; there is little action. The days pass by and same thoughts, same contemplations happen every day and finally one reaches into a state of hypnotic inaction. It is a constant state of fear, anxiety, longing and failure.

Slowly sadness creeps in, as against the target of 'must grow,' I am not growing, I have failed. Sometimes this becomes depression and converts into various disorders. The most significant point to note is inaction – the action stops, and hypnosis persists.

Therefore, if we follow the purpose of the world, which is "you must grow" – the majority of us are going to fall into this 'ideal state' syndrome. In this syndrome, we never reach the ideal state. This will lead to inaction and hypnosis.

But the inquiry into 'I' and "purpose of 'I'" through awareness will give way to intuition, which will define "purpose of 'I'". This purpose is not about growing, most probably it is about solving a problem. Now "solving a problem" is fun and blissful, it has no hierarchy of solving a more significant or a smaller problem. I have chosen what to solve! There cannot be any comparison with self or with the other.

The only next step is to take action towards solving the problem. It could be reading more about it, what has been done about the problem so far, what is the human history of the same?

The knowledge will not just be knowledge; it will be mixed with intuition. It will be like intuitions of past humans and your intuition combining together. Each step is an action, and there is constant action. The action is happening; awareness is happening, fear and anxiety are not happening. The action is happening, it is no longer an effort, as there is no 'must' or 'growth' pressure. Therefore, the 'growth' and 'must' is not, and the action is.

Summary

The Moment is.	
The awareness is.	The time is not.
The 'I' is.	The other is not.
The experience is.	The explanation is not.
The no – 'I' is the one.	The 'I' (social image) is not.
'I' am the purpose.	The purpose is not.
The action is.	The 'growth' and 'must' is not.

❐

8
The Knowing and The Doing

"The logic is not. The game or play is."

If the action is and 'must grow' is not, then it should be straightforward. We just take action, and not focus on 'must' and 'grow.' Logically we should do this, and drop social image and conditioning easily.

But it does not happen. We need a lot of push and pressure to perform, which comes from the word 'must.' Only when we are put under pressure, under the pressure of 'must do', then only we start taking action. Without pressure, we fritter away time and do nothing.

But 'must' puts a lot of pressure and can be disastrous on a personal level or human civilisation level. In the last chapter, we understood how Hitler took 'must grow' too seriously (at any cost). He moved in that direction to reach an utterly insane level.

In a famous movie "Rocky", it is shown how a person goes through tough times and keeps going and wins in the end. The writer of the film is Sylvester Stallone, who himself went through a lot of tough times in his earlier life. The theme of the story is that you must never give up! You must keep moving on! When we watch this kind of movies, we get the motivation of going on and on against all the odds, and keep trying.

It is like doing the impossible act in spite of everything going against you. It is like winning the single big thing for which you waited for your whole life. The final prize is like winning an Oscar and then delivering a speech about how one conquered pain and suffering and kept working hard.

Here is a quote from a documentary "Bigger Stronger Faster":

"He (my dad) was at IBM, for years until he was downsized. But now he has his own business doing taxes. Everybody thinks that success in America is in the number of dollars that you have. And that is not true. The real true heroes are people who go to work every day and do their job and bring up their kids to the best of their ability. But I wanted to be Hulk Hogan. I wanted to be Arnold. I wanted to be Sylvester Stallone."

You may lose your social image, but to drop the hunger of success is not easy. All these awards shows, world titles, Miss Universe contests have got into our heads for years and years. The logic of success is well ingrained in our mind. The important part is to revisit the functioning of mind, which is based on logic.

We should not invest time in concepts like who is the real hero – a man doing a job for 40 years or Rocky Balboa. The point is that there is no hero, heroism has no meaning. There is no hero. The logic of success is based on the concept of a hero. The worldly success means "growth" or "growing" as we understood in the last chapter.

This concept is based on an 'ideal state' – which is not now, which is in the future. The concept of heroism lends great support to the 'ideal state' as to achieve what my hero is doing is the ideal state for me as well. This is a source of constant pain and longing.

We also investigated that a path of 'solving a problem' with our unique gift is a path full of bliss, joy, and sensory experiences. But this logic of mind and world keeps pushing us in the direction of growth and achievement. The concept of a hero is motivating and uplifting from a logical perspective – but it takes the ideal state to a challenging level. This logic creates a lot of despair, burnout and feeling of being cheated at the end. This logic rules the world and is one of the most dangerous mental psychosis in the world.

The action or doing cannot be a product of logic. Just to recap from earlier chapters, logic is a part of the mind's functioning. In the state of awareness, mind disappears, logic disappears, and intuition appears. All our actions are towards achieving some final goal, some objective or being a hero. When hero drops, logic drops, and the ideal state drops, only then can action begin.

The goal should not be to become a VP from a manager. Even to win an Oscar or become the 100m world champion. The goal gives logic to your action, which adds pressure. Here is a quote from the movie 'Watchmen':

"Everyone will die! And the universe will not even notice."

The logic of heroism is based on the importance of being alive. The idea of heroism is that we are born to do something spectacular.

As we have established that we are all unique, it is not a matter of superiority. Even if it is, then we are all equally unique, therefore similarly superior, so the concept of superiority can be laid to rest (since we are 'equally superior').

Nothing is spectacular; spectacular is just a creation of the society or the mind. The things which can be close to spectacular, are awareness, intuition and bliss.

Therefore, heroism comes from 'objective of life' to do something spectacular. What is the importance of winning an Oscar? Acting, singing and running may not be the smartest things a human can do. Why is it that in one country a Rugby player is a hero and in another country Soccer player is a hero? The real point is that there is nothing spectacular. Therefore, there is no hero. There is no concept of an ideal state for ourselves. We do not have to have an objective to 'must grow.' And then there can be action

There is no logic to human life; it is meaningless. There is nothing spectacular about it; there is no hero, there is no ideal state. It may sound repetitive, but this has to be repeated millions of times if required.

The meaninglessness (of life) removes the logic of the mind. The meaninglessness removes the ideal state. The meaninglessness eliminates the hero.

The only meaning to life is to solve a problem with your unique ability through intuition and taking action in awareness. Which is a state of bliss, a state of fun, a state of playing a game! The action is to have fun, to play a game. The game continues.

If you decide that you like to run, then you should focus on running. But what problem are you solving with running? You want to run fast, that is the problem you are solving. Does winning matter? It may or it may not! Go and win, enjoy winning in your backyard, enjoy winning in the Olympic stadium – it should be the same.

The words of logic are 'finally,' 'in the end' – 'there was a victory.' In reality, finally and in the end we are dead. Chasing that final victory can be very painful. This logic comes from knowledge, and from previous learnings. Therefore, it is repetitive. The most negative impact of the repetitive nature of past knowledge is repetition of pain, again and again for the same issues.

What does it mean to drop the knowledge or the logic?

As per our past knowledge, a snake can bite, and that bite can kill a human being. Should I drop this learning and try to touch the snake and gather new learning? Some people have made it their profession to catch snakes, others to study snakes and produce documentaries and TV shows. But it does not mean, that everyone should catch snakes. The people who catch snakes, had an intuition, had an internal urge to do it. That was their unique calling.

But what should I do? Run away as soon as I see the snake? Be careful not to go near the snake? Should I use previous learning or not?

These are important questions, which need to be investigated. The knowledge of the past can come to me through another human being, a book, a TV show, a movie and so on. The knowledge of past may be intuition or a fact or a deception. I should agree to analyse the knowledge of the past. I should also decide to accept a fact – as the fact is absolute. But it is not what the knowledge of past has put forward, it is my state of awareness, which will help me choose from knowledge of past. My state of awareness and playfulness should look at knowledge – and decide to accept or reject it. What I accept, it becomes a fact, what I reject is the deceptive logic system. The fact is absolute. This is also an action and combined with intuition, this becomes exciting and blissful.

It is established that a snake can bite and kill. First, it was established that a snake has 'something' which it puts into our blood stream through its fangs. Later it was established that 'something' is venom. The venom needs to be studied, therefore, a snake needed to be caught.

There were ways and means established to catch the snake. These learnings may have taken several generations of humans.

These are facts, and if one is solving a problem, one has to provide the next piece of the puzzle. Several generations of humans may complete the puzzle.

This state is relevant, and the state has to be playful. In the playful state, the logic disappears, facts appear, intuitions appear through which the next piece of the puzzle appears – which is the action or the doing. Therefore, the logic is not, the game or the play is.

Summary

The Moment is.	
The awareness is.	The time is not.
The 'I' is.	The other is not.
The experience is.	The explanation is not.
The no– 'I' is the one.	The 'I' (social image) is not.
'I' am the purpose.	The purpose is not.
The action is.	The 'growth' and 'must' is not.
The game or the play is.	The logic is not.

9
The Suffering and The Ignorance

"The life is not. The death is not. The silence is."

There is constant suffering in being alive, and there is constant fear in the concept of death. For a living person, there could only be "concept of death," not the experience of death. The 'constant suffering' is part of being a human being and part of being alive. The 'suffering' is a matter of fact rather than a conclusion from the analysis.

Most people in the world go through suffering, and they accept or avoid suffering as part of life. We have understood in earlier chapters that we need to investigate pain and suffering. It is generally said, 'there are good times, and there are bad times,'. Therefore suffering is accepted or it is avoided by accepting hope.

Human beings have a tough life, it has been like that for ages. Right from the early ages, humans had to hunt, farm and make other arrangements to stay alive. In the current era, man has to solve many more problems than just arranging for food.

In addition to health problems, there are relationship problems, financial problems and so on. As understood earlier, chasing the 'ideal state' is a cause of suffering.

Generally speaking, the concept of death lends fear. The idea of death is sometimes helpful in removal of 'day to day' suffering for a short while. If we go to a funeral, we forget about all the stress and drop the suffering for some time. We think about death and tell ourselves since I am going to die one day, why should I suffer? The concept of death is full of fear.

When a person thinks seriously about death, one keeps wondering what will happen after death, will I be able to see my loved ones? What will become of me after death?

Some people may claim, that "suffering is good if there is a good enough reason for it." This good enough reason may be religion, advertisements and media, or being a hero in a situation. These people have sincerely accepted suffering as part of life. Therefore, they no longer understand it.

It is so unfortunate that religion, nationalism and advertising have blinded people so much that they are not even able to recognise that they are suffering. Life has become a relative measure, "I am better than him and worse than him, but at least I am better than most."

These people who have completely immersed themselves into psychosis and societal conditioning, fall into deep depression and related problems when the situations and circumstances are against them. For example, there are corporate firms in which being shouted upon by the manager is well accepted, even getting abused is well accepted.

It gets worse for senior-level positions, where vice presidents and directors are ready to take any treatment to protect their big houses and lavish vacations. You may notice that the poor people or people doing the lowest forms of jobs do not accept this kind of treatment.

To look 'sexy,' girls are starving themselves to achieve a particular thin look. As per a survey in London, 40% of girls aged 14 and 15 do not eat breakfast to stay thin or become thin.

This is motivated by skinny models and actresses, who are their role models. The suffering of not eating is well accepted. The result of this acceptance of pain is that in the modern world, the human being is becoming hedonic and committing plunder. Sex, food, alcohol, and showing-off have become the focus of life. All of this is to escape from suffering, but escape is required since the pain is accepted as a part of life.

As per surveys in the USA, over 35% adults are obese, and 17% of children are obese. The reasons for this situation are fat and carbohydrate-rich junk food, sugary drinks, and habits of snacking all day. But the real reason is acceptance of suffering, just like starving is accepted, overeating is accepted. Food has become a remedy for sufferings, it is like "Since I am not feeling well, let me treat myself to a triple sundae."

Even sex has become weird, rather than actual sex, there is a lot of noise about sex, women and men trying to look provocative and a whole industry around that has become more popular. It has led to multiple problems, with rape being the biggest problem. Sex has become a monster of an issue, with no meaning and no direction.

Here is a quote from Frederic Bastiat:

"Society is composed of men, and every man is a free agent. Since man is free, he can choose; since he can choose, he can err; since he can err, he can suffer. I go further: He must err, and he must suffer; for his starting point is ignorance."

Let us focus on the fact that suffering is there. You may try to live life in any way possible; there is bound to be 'suffering.' Expectations, Money, relationships, societal image, health issues and many other things are going to contribute to 'suffering.' After that comes shopping, clubbing, drinking, eating, sex and other means to avoid suffering.

On the other side is the concept of death, which is considered to be the highest form of fear. Unlike suffering, death is not accepted – it is avoided all the time. Thinking about death contributes to fear and sadness. At times, death is accepted, but even that is a trick and an escape, an escape from other sufferings of life.

Running away from life is running away from suffering – which is normal. Therefore, let's accept the feeling of escape. The sense of escape should not be looked at as some kind of failure; it may be well received. One must accept feelings of escapism as normal feelings as life is suffering.

Escape from suffering by using the 'concept of death' may also be an acceptable idea. The idea of death removes the misery of life. Pain is eliminated by the fear of death. Death is perceived as the biggest suffering one can have. Therefore, the fear of death is the fear of highest suffering. This fear of most significant suffering removes smaller sufferings. For a living person, fear of death as suffering may beat other miseries like not being able to succeed at the job. The point is that, life is suffering, and death, is the biggest suffering. We try to remove smaller sufferings by introducing a bigger suffering.

Death is accepted to remove the daily sufferings of life, but this is a trick. A trick to avoid the misery of life. Rather than investigating and resolving our pains, the method is to bring the 'concept of death' – and all sufferings will disappear for a little while. After some time, we start doing the same activities again.

Sometimes, life becomes significant suffering, may be a significant health problem or a relationship failure. This suffering may be so significant, that the person comes face to face with the pain.

This is a dangerous moment, as with a fragile self, which is habituated to avoid suffering – this moment could be hazardous. These moments can be pivotal, and as understood earlier these can become moments of awareness where a person can see the absolute. But at the same time, these moments can result in suicidal tendencies.

The concepts of life and death can be related to suffering. One tries to remove one pain by introducing the other, or by trying to escape the pain with hedonic measures. This is the ignorance of human beings.

Life and death cannot be resolved; this is the ignorance which creates the suffering. The resolution as a concept seeks a permanent solution. Life is transitory; life is always changing – the types of pains are continually evolving. Death is just a concept, and thoughts about death are always avoided as death is the biggest suffering. It is impossible to resolve something which one avoids all the time. If one does try to address death, it can be a more fruitful exercise than resolving life.

The attempts to resolve life or death must disappear. Using the 'concept of death' to remove other sufferings must disappear. It is not important to ask questions like "What is life?" We have understood the more important questions, which are on lines of "Who am 'I'?".

With playfulness, the attempt of resolution can disappear. With awareness and experience, one may be able to focus from moment to moment. This focus from moment to moment can be understood as counting each breath.

The counting of breaths can be a peaceful exercise. It is the understanding that each breath is a distinct moment. Once our concepts of life and death are dropped, suffering becomes clear. This clarity gives rise to the resolution of pain, which is silence. Here, silence is a verb. It is a moment to moment silence. No thought (the question of mind) can be adequately answered, and thought is the starting point of psychosis. Silence is required, which may come with awareness and playfulness. The absence of thought is silence.

The silence is transitory just like life. If it is there, there is a focus on some action. The easiest way of achieving silence is to focus on breathing.

Breathing is our core activity, the focus on this activity is natural, and silence can be achieved. Focus on breathing in and breathing out. Between breathing in and breathing out, there is a small point, where you are neither breathing in nor breathing out. You may focus on this point and achieve silence; this is a meditation technique taught by Lord Shiva (Hindu God) in Vigyan bhairav tantra.

In the moment of silence, you are free from suffering. At that moment you are aware. Therefore, you are not ignorant. Thus, the life and death are not. The silence is.

Summary

The Moment is.	
The awareness is.	The time is not.
The 'I' is.	The other is not.
The experience is.	The explanation is not.
The no – 'I' is the one.	The 'I' (social image) is not.
'I' am the purpose.	The purpose is not.
The action is.	The 'growth' and 'must' is not.
The game or the play is.	The logic is not.

❑

10
The Love and The Beloved

"The lover is not. The gratitude is."

Investigating love is important. The moment of awareness can give rise to intuition. A moment of silence (with only focus on breathing) can give rise to the flowering of love. Love may be generated out of a moment of silence.

But to consider that love can only be generated via the moment of silence is wrong. Love is spontaneous; it is produced on its own, or due to some incident or accident. Love can convert into awareness, bliss, joy, intuition and silence. Love is the most natural path to awareness and bliss. Love can turn into silence if love is for god or nature or the existence.

There is no science in the creation of love, it just happens. The moment of silence may be a starting point for love. But there is no guarantee for that.

This love does not mean the love between a man and a woman; this is just love. This love is characterized by giving and enjoying the fact that what you have given is accepted and appreciated by the other. Love is most easily understood as love of a parent for a young child. If the parent brings a toy for the young child and the child accepts the toy and starts playing with it, the parent feels most satisfied. This love has no reciprocation; nothing is received in return. Just that your gift of love is well received is the ultimate reward.

The word we can use is gratitude. Gratitude is a word used to show appreciation for what we have been given. Here gratitude means that our love has been accepted and enjoyed. The word gratitude will seem right when we understand love.

Love is for the beloved; it is the constant desire to make the beloved happy. It is the continuous effort to serve the beloved, any amount of serving is not enough. In love, one wants to give more and more. There is no question of receiving or reciprocation. Only giving and giving.

The beloved is the only real thing, the lover disappears. For the lover, the lover is no more, only the beloved is. The ecstasy is in giving the love and serving the beloved. The joy is the happiness of the beloved. The ecstasy is there if my gift is accepted and enjoyed by the beloved.

The beloved can be a god or the almighty or nature or the existence. In that case, love becomes poetry, music, songs and other forms of art. Since there is no direct person to receive the love, it converts into different types of creative expression. The artistic expression also blossoms in case of the beloved being a human being.

But in the case of a human being, the love can be given in various forms directly to the beloved.

In case, the love is for something inanimate, love blossoms in the abstract.

This love is madness and is not well understood and appreciated by society. Love kills the lover, and only the beloved is left. Therefore, love is the most natural path to bliss. But it may be the toughest as you cannot push love. The silence can bring love to the surface. Silence could be one path to the flowering of love.

The impressive part of love is the dissolution of the lover. The lover dissolves into the beloved. The beloved's happiness is happiness, the beloved's sadness is sadness. But when the beloved is the nature or the god, the human dissolves into nature. The human wants to contribute to each entity in nature. Anyone's joy becomes the lover's joy. Anyone's pain becomes the lover's pain. All flowers bloom for the lover; it can be a state of endless bliss. For example, the Sufi saints experience this kind of love.

Now how can anyone achieve this? Is there a process? Yes.

The process can be initiated with silence. It is not a sure shot process, but it may work. The silence can be the path to love.

There are various ways to understand the surrogates of love. One big proxy of love as we know is only giving and not expecting. Since the lover has dissolved, there is no question of wanting and expecting? The lover is not there. The other surrogate of love as we understand is the gratitude if the beloved accepts the gift of love.

The third surrogate of love is 'to drop effortlessly'. Once the moment of silence happens, and the flowering of love occurs. One starts dropping all kinds of issues effortlessly. This is the beauty of love.

This happens because process disappears, ego disappears, purpose disappears, and only the beloved remains. And the gratitude remains.

This gratitude is full of joy and bliss. It is the joy of witnessing the beloved enjoying your gift of love. Therefore, the lover is not. The gratitude is.

Summary

The Moment is.

The awareness is.	The time is not.
The 'I' is.	The other is not.
The experience is.	The explanation is not.
The no – 'I' is the one.	The 'I' (social image) is not.
'I' am the purpose.	The purpose is not.
The action is.	The 'growth' and 'must' is not.
The game or the play is.	The logic is not.

❐

11
The Money and The Nature

"The Greed is not. The scarcity is not. Nature is."

The gratitude has to be understood further. The sunlight, the air we breathe, the rivers, the seas, the oceans, the plants and the animals do not belong to the human beings. Human beings do not create them. These are all gifts of nature for us. Instead, these can be considered as the love of life.

We, humans, love nature as well. We like to be close to nature; we visit mountains, rivers, lakes, beaches, forests to gain peace and bliss. There is a definite connection between nature and us, in simple words, we are part of nature. We are a subset of nature. Some humans may think that nature is the subset of humans, which is not correct.

We understand the gratitude of love. Gratitude that someone has accepted my gift of love. Nature has provided for all creatures all the necessary facilities to stay alive.

Humans cannot create most of nature's gifts, and these are critical to the survival of human and other living organisms. Therefore, there should be constant gratitude towards nature.

Also, we have processes going on in our bodies, which are beyond the voluntary control of the human brain. Can you command your liver functioning or kidney functioning? No. Should we have some gratitude towards the kidneys, liver, and other body organs? Thank you for continually functioning all day and all night!

Man has created buildings, air conditioners, cars and so many great things, in addition to the gifts of nature. Today one can enjoy both gifts of nature and gifts created by human beings.

The gifts of nature are still free in some manner. The creations of human beings have to be purchased with money.

Money is a method of transaction. It is a universal way to deal with goods and services. Money making has become a big paranoia. The majority of discussions and talk in life is about making money and related things like job, business, investments, stock markets, real estate and so on. It is highly overrated.

There is no problem in making money if you solve other problems. Money making has to be a transactional process, and sometimes a creative process driven by intuition. But overall it is a small issue and can be easily tackled.

Money making has become a high-pressure process, but the reason it has become such a stressful thing is that there is so much discussion over it. Therefore, we may assume that it is not difficult to make money and it is just there to allow us to make necessary transactions in life. We need fundamental human facilities, for which money making is not a problem. Here is a quote from Adam Smith, the father of capitalism:

"Labour was the first price, the original purchase – money that was paid for all things. It was not by gold or by silver, but by labour that all wealth of the world was originally purchased."

It is very important to understand, that money is a mechanism for movement or transaction of goods and services created by labour. Most people think money has some more significant purpose other than purchasing things. Therefore, the concept of effort or labour towards an objective is more important than money.

Even if it might seem that all labour is done to earn money, money is a byproduct of labour.

Here is an interesting quote by Karl Marx, father of communism and socialism:

"The writer must earn money to live and to write, but he must by no means live and write for the purpose of making money."

The concept of money kills the idea of gratitude. Gratitude for money is there, until a basic level of existence. But once a person starts hoarding money, and there is competition, there is no gratitude.

There is only greed. Greed can kill the gratitude. Today with widespread greed, the basic gratitude is missing.

Greed is the feeling of scarcity all the time. Greed is the best friend of ego; they go together. And both greed and ego are enemies of gratitude. "I am superior, and I want more."

On the other side, one may say, I am in love, and I hope my love is accepted. If my love is approved, I will be grateful – that is gratitude. It is tough to say, if my money is received, I will be grateful. If money is paid to me, I may be grateful, but there is no gratitude while giving money. Money and fame, which is greed and ego, have corrupted the human being. This corruption has taken one away from gratitude.

Gratitude as a trait is slowly diminishing. Since gratitude is missing, there is fake love. Fake love is calculative – what have you given me and how much I should give back.

To understand gratitude one must appreciate nature. Nature is the true lover, as it is always the giver. To understand gratitude, one has to thank the nature for providing sunlight, for providing air and water. To understand gratitude, one has to appreciate the natural processes happening in the human body, which is keeping a person alive. To understand gratitude, one must thank the natural process of formation of a baby in the womb.

Greed is not just related to money; it is related to land, it is related to a position, it is related to power, it is related to recognition and it is also related to sex. There is greed for recognition; any amount is not good enough. There is greed for sex; any amount is not good enough.

A greedy person can never enjoy love, music, poetry, art or silence. Greed is very dangerous; it pushes all joy and bliss into the future. When I have this, then I will be happy. Any amount of money, sex, recognition will not be enough.

Gratitude brings happiness and bliss to now. Gratitude starts with nature, where we have received so many gifts without any expectation. Gratitude is the door to understanding and experience love. Gratitude is real, as we have so many gifts, due to the love of nature.

Gratitude is now, which is the gateway to love and bliss. And the core source of gratitude is nature. Therefore, the greed is not. The scarcity is not. Nature is.

Summary

The Moment is.	
The awareness is.	The time is not.
The 'I' is.	The other is not.
The experience is.	The explanation is not.
The no-'I' is the one.	The 'I' (social image) is not.
'I' am the purpose.	The purpose is not.
The action is.	The 'growth' and 'must' is not.
Thc game or the play is.	The logic is not.

12
A Walk in The Park

"Is."

In an elementary class of English, while teaching the concept of 'sentence', one of the students asked the teacher, "A dying soldier asking for water says 'water,' it that a sentence?" The teacher replied "yes." One word can be a sentence. The one word is "Is."

As per one scientific theory, there was a Big Bang, a big explosion which signifies crucial early development of the universe. Now the whole universe is expanding; it is referred to as redshift. The galaxies are moving away from each other. This theory was a result of work of various scientists and was based on the general Theory of Relativity. The other theory of the universe is the Steady State theory, which agrees that universe is expanding but it is always the same and it has no beginning or end. The Steady State theory got discredited over time, and its calculations did not work out with the general Theory of Relativity as well. The Big Bang Theory, on the other hand, argued that universe is finite.

Here is a quote from Stephen Hawking:

"We do not yet have a good theoretical understanding of the observations that the expansion of the universe is accelerating again, after a long period of slowing down. Without such an understanding, we cannot be sure of the future of the universe. Will it continue to expand forever? Is inflation a law of Nature? Or will the universe eventually collapse again? New observational results and theoretical advances are coming in rapidly. Cosmology is a very exciting and active subject. We are getting close to answering the age-old questions. Why are we here? Where did we come from?"

The origin of the universe is one of the most interesting questions. This question is intriguing, this question comes up, especially when we see the night sky with stars. But we can also think of a similar issue looking at a beautiful new green leaf in a plant – how did this beautiful thing originate? It is not the question of the origin of life as a whole. The question is only about that beautiful leaf.

The answer for the origin of the universe could be the Big Bang theory. It may be proven after some years that the Big Bang Theory was wrong and there is some other theory to explain all of this. Stephen Hawking has said that we are getting close to answering these questions.

As per our understanding from the last chapter, nature gives us so many gifts. Nature makes all the arrangements for our survival. We are all part of nature. We (human beings) have originated as nature facilitated our origination. We are one of the millions of organisms in the world.

Each one has developed as explained by Darwin's Theory of Evolution. But this development and evolution are dependent upon our planet's atmosphere and conditions.

Big Bang theory, Darwin's theory, and Einstein's theories are explanations of nature, universe and existence. These theories are not foundations or reasons of origin. The universe or the flower cannot be recreated despite all these theories. The theories are meaningful and logical and have contributed to great scientific developments.

But the Big bang theory cannot alter the speed of expansion of the universe. The universe is as it is. The flower is as it is. The leaf is as it is. Nature is as it is. We are part of nature. Therefore 'I' is as it is.

Nature is the starting point of everything. Nature is the ultimate force. You can call it God, you can call it Almighty, you can call it Jesus or Allah or Krishna or anything. Here we will refer to it as nature. Nature is absolute; it has no meaning. There could be an explanation of nature, as in "how" of nature, but not "why" and "who started" nature.

Each of the religions has tried to explain "why" and "who started" the natures. Each religion claims that their god created the universe and their god created human, the most superior being. Each religion claims that it is the only religion and its god is the supreme. Each of the religious books has tens of theories on how and why the world was created, and apparently, it was designed by their god.

The concept of religion may be relevant to human race. But the explanations of the universe do not seem right. The idea of god is used to create order in the human race. A lot of people are using these concepts only for personal profits.

The idea of god and concept of nature is similar, therefore, can be used interchangeably. But nature is real; the universe is real, the flower is real, air is real, water is real, the mountain is real – therefore not an abstract concept. Nature is.

Human beings are part of nature. Human beings are just like the other living beings. Human beings are not superior to other living beings. Nature does not differentiate between the living and the non-living, everything is an equal part of nature. These are the characteristics of nature, which cannot be challenged. Therefore, the human being is neither superior nor more important. No religion is superior to the other; no one god is superior to the other and god did not create the universe. We may say that God is the universe, and the universe is the nature. God, universe, and nature are interchangeable.

But this god, universe, and nature do not have feelings, emotions or a character. It is not happy, not sad, not angry, not anything at all. It just is. And it is the giver, it is the facilitator, and everything is part of it. Human beings are part of it.

But human beings are happy, sad, angry, insulted, stressed, respected, rewarded and so on. But our superset, which is nature, does not have any such characteristics. How did humans become like this? Have we lost our way? Maybe we have!

The obvious thing for humans is to be one with nature. There is only one thing to do, to be like nature. This can also be understood as being one with nature or universe or god. When we have the same characteristics as nature, we and nature are one. And actually, we are born one. Nature and ‘I’ are one. You are nature and nature, is you.

There is no plan for nature. There should be no plan for a human. Nature does not experience any stress. Human should not experience any stress.

Nature is. The ‘I’ is. Nature and ‘I’ is the same. Therefore, the universe, nature, god, humans and each of the living and non-living thing is. It leads us to the one-word sentence which signifies the oneness and the ultimate unity of everything. Is.

Now let us go for a walk in the park.

Summary

The Moment is.	
The awareness is.	The time is not.
The ‘I’ is.	The other is not.
The experience is.	The explanation is not.
The no – ‘I’ is the one.	The ‘I’ (social image) is not.
‘I’ am the purpose.	The purpose is not.
The action is.	The ‘growth’ and ‘must’ is not.
The game or the play is.	The logic is not.